MW00876491

This journal belongs to :

Made in the USA
Las Vegas, NV
16 July 2024

92408439R00056